B...
A...
S0-AQE-107

Lexile Value: 1230L

D1520443

Terror, INC.

BOKO HARAM

EARLE RICE JR.

Mitchell Lane
PUBLISHERS
**2001 SW 31st Avenue
Hallandale, FL 33009
www.mitchelllane.com**

Printing   1   2   3   4   5   6   7   8

Al-Qaeda
Boko Haram
Hamas

Hezbollah
Islamic State
Muslim Brotherhood

ABOUT THE COVER: The cover image, taken from a video filmed by Boko Haram in 2014, features its Islamist leader Abubakar Shekau, unmasked in the center. Like most terrorists, the followers of Shekau shown here are masked to hide their identities and instill fear in their victims. In August 2016, the group's newspaper *al-Nadaa* announced Abu Musab al-Barnawi was the new leader of Boko Haram. Shekau's standing in the group remains unclear.

ABOUT THE AUTHOR: Earle Rice Jr. is a former senior design engineer and technical writer in the aerospace, electronic-defense, and nuclear industries. He has devoted full time to his writing since 1993, specializing in military and counterinsurgency subjects. Earle is the author of more than 80 published books. He is listed in *Who's Who in America* and is a member of the Society of Children's Book Writers and Illustrators, the League of World War I Aviation Historians, the Air Force Association, and the Disabled American Veterans.

Library of Congress Cataloging-in-Publication Data
Names: Rice, Earle, author.
Title: Boko Haram / by Earle Rice Jr.
Description: Hallandale, FL : Mitchell Lane Publishers, [2018] | Series: Terror INC |
    Audience: Age: 9-13. | Includes bibliographical references and index.
Identifiers: LCCN 2017009122 | ISBN 9781680200492 (library bound)
Subjects: LCSH: Boko Haram. | Terrorist organizations—Nigeria. | Insurgency—Nigeria.
Classification: LCC HV6433.N62 B67 2017 | DDC 363.32509669—dc23
LC record available at https://lccn.loc.gov/2017009122

eBook ISBN: 978-1-68020-050-8

Contents

Foreword 4

CHAPTER 1   Lives at Risk 7
                The World Reacts 13

CHAPTER 2   Turning to Violence 15
                Mayhem in Maiduguri 19

CHAPTER 3   Waging War on Infidels 21
                Abubakar Shekau 25

CHAPTER 4   Caught Between Two Evils 27
                A House Divided 31

CHAPTER 5   Targeting Westerners 33
                Dying Hard 39

Timeline 40
Chapter Notes 42
Principal People 44
Glossary 45
Further Reading 46
Works Consulted 46
On the Internet 47
Index 48

Words in **bold** throughout can be found in the Glossary.

Foreword

Terror has plagued the world since men in caves flailed away at each other with sticks and stones. As the world emerged from **primeval** times and entered the ancient age, humans clashed on a larger, more advanced scale called warfare. Slings, arrows, and spears wrought havoc in the Golden Age of Greece and stained the glory that was Rome. Ethnic and religious strife followed close behind. In medieval times, crusading Christians and faith-based Muslims carved a bloody path across the Middle East with sword, lance, and scimitar in the causes of God and Allah. Americans engaged in "total war" for the first time during the Civil War, a war pitting brother against brother and fathers against sons at a cost of 750,000 lives. The 20th century introduced global wars that claimed the lives of tens of millions of combatants and civilians.

Today, international terrorism has become a form of warfare. The U.S. Department of Defense defines terrorism as "the unlawful use of—or threatened use of—force or violence against individuals or property to **coerce** or intimidate governments or societies, often to achieve political, religious, or ideological objectives." In many parts of the world, terror is a way of life. Militant Muslim extremists seek to rid Muslim countries of what they view as the **profane** influence of the West and replace their governments with fundamentalist regimes based on their interpretation of the religion of **Islam**.

The American way of life changed forever when 19 Islamist terrorists flew fuel-laden aircraft—flying bombs—into the World Trade Center in New York City and the Pentagon in Washington,

Students in Lagos, Nigeria, support the worldwide #BringBackOurGirls movement to commemorate the first anniversary of the abduction of Chibok schoolgirls by Boko Haram terrorists.

DC, on September 11, 2001. Today, radical Islamist groups continue to be America's main threat of terrorism.

It should be noted that only a small minority of Muslims believe in terror as a strategy. A recent Gallup poll indicated that just seven percent of the world's 1.6 billion Muslims support extremist views of terrorism. The purpose of this book is to alert and enlighten the reader about that seven percent, while affirming the essential righteousness of the other 93 percent of Islam's followers. Peace be upon the gentle of mind, spirit, and deed.

On April 14, 2014, Boko Haram militants rumbled into the town of Chibok, Nigeria, and seized nearly 300 schoolgirls in the dark of night. The group's leader, Abubakar Shekau, later threatened to sell the girls into slavery if imprisoned Boko Haram members were not released. The two girls seen here escaped their captors by jumping off a truck, Joy Bishara (left) and Hadiza Fali.

CHAPTER 1
Lives at Risk

They came to Chibok in the warm spring night of April 14-15, 2014. They came bearing Kalashnikov AK-47 assault rifles and RPGs (rocket-propelled grenades). They came wearing **camos** and claiming to be government soldiers. They came on a mission later described by Great Britain's Prime Minister David Cameron as "an act of pure evil."[1] And they came to abduct and enslave nearly 300 schoolgirls from the primarily Christian village in northeastern Nigeria. They were members of Boko Haram (BOH-koh hah-RAHM). Boko Haram is an Islamic militant movement based in northeastern Nigeria. Its members are intent upon establishing an Islamic state in a country divided roughly equally between Muslims and Christians. On this night, they quickly shed their assumed identities as government soldiers with cries of "Allahu Akbar! (God is Great!)," followed by the charade-ending announcement of "We are Boko Haram!"[2] They punctuated their **revelatory** remarks with staccato bursts into the air from their Kalashnikovs and raucous death threats.

Moments earlier, Boko Haram had rumbled into town in trucks and parked outside the Chibok Government Girls Secondary School. They had been targeting schools since 2010, killing hundreds of students and keeping thousands more from attending classes. A spokesman for the terrorist group vowed they would continue their attacks as long as the Nigerian government persisted in interfering with traditional Islamic education. Boko Haram means "Western education is forbidden" or "Western education is sinful." They believed Western education undermined

Islamic teachings and their ultimate goal of establishing an Islamic state.

Because of declining security conditions, the Chibok school had been closed for the past four weeks. Tonight, however, hundreds of female students ranging in age from 16 to 18 from multiple area schools had been summoned to take final exams in physics. Their presence afforded Boko Haram a prime opportunity to continue their spread of violence.

The terrorists swarmed off their trucks and stormed into the classrooms amid the frightened shrieks and screams of the schoolgirls. "We woke up and we saw people in military uniforms,"[3] recalled Kuma Ishaku. Kuma, a soft-spoken 18-year-old wearing a bright white blouse with silver sparkles, was one of a number of students from outlying areas who were sleeping at the school that night. They awoke to the sound of gunfire. She went on: "They were telling us: 'Come, come. We are army.'"[4] Some of the girls did not believe them and resisted.

The intruders said, "If you want to die, sit down here. We will kill you. If you don't want to die, you will enter the trucks."[5] Terrified and sobbing, 276 girls filed out of the school and boarded the trucks. While confusion reigned, Kuma managed to escape into the semi-desert scrub. Others, like Joy Bishara, jumped from the trucks while en route to Boko Haram campsites in the nearby **Sambisa Forest**.

"Yes, yes, I ran into the bush," said Joy, a tall 18-year-old in a brown T-shirt labeled "Ice Box," recalling her numbed reasoning that night. "I don't know where I'm going. I think they will kill me. They were telling us, 'We will kill you.'"[6]

"They told us: 'We are Boko Haram. We will burn your school. You shall not do school again,'" Joy continued. "'You shall do Islamic school.' And they were shouting, 'Allahu Akbar!' 'God is great!'"[7] To ensure the girls would "not do school again" in Chibok, Boko Haram burned down the schoolhouse. They also put the

Early in their reign of terror, Boko Haram Islamists established their base of operations in the Sambisa Forest in northeastern Nigeria's Borno State. They operated successfully out of this forest stronghold for several years, killing untold thousands of victims. In 2016, at year's end, the government forces of new President Muhammadu Buhari—a few of whom are shown here—finally succeeded in driving Boko Haram out of their forest hideout.

torch to numerous homes. Their work done, they boarded their trucks with their teenage prisoners and rumbled out of town toward destinations unknown. Besides Kuma and Joy, 55 other girls either escaped that night or in the following weeks. The other 219 remained in captivity.

In this image drawn from a Boko Haram video, the Nigerian terrorists affirm their capture of the Chibok schoolgirls allegedly shown here on Monday, May 12, 2014. Early in 2017, government soldiers recovered one of the Chibok girls, along with her baby, but many others still remain in captivity.

The kidnapping shocked the world. It also achieved instant worldwide notoriety for Boko Haram. Three weeks after the abduction of the girls, the worst fears of their parents appeared to be realized.

On May 5, 2014, a man claiming to be Boko Haram leader Abubakar Shekau released a video in which he claimed, "I abducted your girls. I will sell them in the market, by Allah. There is a market for selling humans. Allah says I should sell. He commands me to sell. I will sell women. I sell women."[8] And the world reacted.

In an address to a **philanthropic** gathering in New York City two days later, former Secretary of State Hillary Clinton condemned the abductions: "The seizure of these young women by this radical extremist group, Boko Haram, is abominable. It's criminal, it's an act of terrorism and it really merits the fullest response possible—first and foremost from the government of Nigeria."[9]

While delivering the weekly presidential radio and internet address on May 10, First Lady Michelle Obama said that she and President Barack Obama were both "outraged and heartbroken." She added, "This unconscionable act was committed by a terrorist group determined to keep these girls from getting an education—grown men attempting to snuff out the aspirations of young girls."[10]

First Lady Michele Obama frowns while displaying a hashtag sign with an international plea to #BringBackOurGirls to support the recovery of the abducted Chibok girls.

On May 9, 2014, some 20 people with makeshift signs rallied in Washington, DC, in support of the schoolgirls kidnapped by Boko Haram militant extremists. The rally, organized by Amnesty International and other human rights groups, was held 24 days after the girls were abducted.

In an effort to put viral pressure on Nigerian authorities to recover the girls, a campaign labeled with the globally trending hashtag #BringBackOurGirls was started on several websites. Numerous notable figures endorsed it. Crowds from New York to London rallied in its cause.

Shekau answered the international outcry with a demand for the release of imprisoned Boko Haram members: "I swear to almighty Allah, you will not see [the girls] again until you release our brothers that you have captured."[11]

On May 11, Nigerian President Goodluck Jonathan pledged, "Wherever these girls are, we will get them out."[12] Meanwhile, their lives would hang in the balance.

The World Reacts

On May 6, 2014, the United States government announced it was sending a team to Nigeria to help in the search for the missing schoolgirls of Chibok. In an interview with NBC News that same day, President Obama said, "We're going to do everything we can to provide assistance to them." He noted that it was a "terrible situation."[13]

On May 14 in London, British Prime Minister David Cameron told Parliament that Britain was sending surveillance aircraft to Nigeria. It would also send a team to assist the Nigerian army, and another to work with U.S. experts in analyzing information on the location of the girls.

Three days later, French President François Hollande hosted a security summit meeting in Paris. He noted, "Boko Haram is an organization that is linked to terrorism in Africa and whose will is to destabilize the north of Nigeria, certainly, and all the neighboring countries of Nigeria and beyond that region."[14] At the conclusion of the meeting, he announced a plan for Nigeria and four neighboring countries to share intelligence and border surveillance in the hunt for the girls.

But despite the world's best efforts, more than 200 of them still remain missing as of mid-2017.

A group of some 270 schoolgirls in Wellington, New Zealand protest the abduction of their sister Nigerian schoolgirls on May 14, 2014. The protesters marched to the Parliament grounds.

Catfish provide one of the staples of the Nigerian diet. Nigerian youths often buy the fish from local markets in Abuja, the national capital, and resell them to turn a profit.

CHAPTER 2
Turning to Violence

Boko Haram gained worldwide notoriety by kidnapping the schoolgirls and threatening to sell them into slavery. Its victimization of innocent young girls shocked even the most hardened observers of terrorist activities. The kidnappings represented the latest in a long line of violent incidents orchestrated by Boko Haram fighters in Nigeria since 2009. And it marked a new low in Nigeria's long and turbulent history.

Nigeria traces its roots back hundreds of years ago to several ancient kingdoms. Some of them became important cultural and trading centers. In the modern era, the United Kingdom gained control of Nigeria in the late 1800s and early 1900s. Britain claimed Nigeria as a colony and **protectorate** until it gained independence in 1960. It is now officially known as the Federal Republic of Nigeria.

Located just above the Equator on the coast of West Africa, Nigeria is a land of great diversity. Its terrain features range from hot, rainy wetlands to dry, sandy deserts, grassy plains, and tropical forests, with high plateaus and mountains rising in some parts of the country. Nigeria's population of an estimated 178 million people—including more than 250 ethnic groups—ranks it as Africa's most densely populated nation and the seventh most populated in the world.

Many Nigerians earn their living farming, fishing, or herding, and rich oil deposits have brought new wealth to the nation in recent times. About half its people live in rural areas, but Nigeria also has several large, crowded cities. Lagos, on the coast, is its chief commercial center; Abuja, centrally located, is its capital.

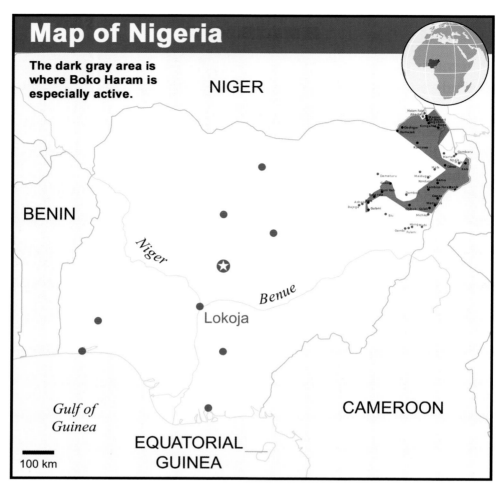

Map of Nigeria

The dark gray area is where Boko Haram is especially active.

NIGER

BENIN

Niger

Benue

Lokoja

Gulf of Guinea

CAMEROON

EQUATORIAL GUINEA

100 km

After Nigeria gained independence in 1960, military leaders controlled it from 1966 to 1979. A civilian administration governed from 1979 to 1983. Military leaders regained control in 1983. Civilian government was restored in 1999.

Most Nigerians are black Africans. Of their more than 250 ethnic groups, the three largest groups are, in order of size, the Hausa, the Yoruba, and the Igbo. They account for about 70 percent of Nigeria's population. The Hausa live mostly in northern Nigeria as farmers, craftworkers, and traders. Most Yoruba live in cities in the southwestern part of the country and farm the land in the surrounding countryside. The Igbo form the bulk of the population in southeastern Nigeria. Many of them have adapted to the Western way of life and work in business and government.

While English is the official language of Nigeria, each ethnic group has its own distinct language. About half the people are Muslims, who reside primarily in the north. Christians compose about 40 percent of the population and live mainly in the southern and central parts of the country. The distinctly different lifestyles of the north and the south, coupled with a widening economic disparity between the impoverished north and the more prosperous south, have given rise to ethnic, religious, and political tensions in Nigeria since 1999. Boko Haram grew out of such tensions.

In 2002, a Muslim leader named Mohammed Yusuf founded Boko Haram in Maiduguri, the capital of the northeastern state of Borno. At its inception, the movement took the name *Jama'atu Ahlis Sunna Lidda'awati wal-Jihad*, or "People Committed to the **Propagation** of the Prophet's Teachings and Jihad."[1] The name "Boko Haram" is a Hausa/Arabic name and implies a rejection of Western civilizations and institutions. The shortened name was later popularized by the media but rejected by the movement's members, who prefer the original long-form name.

Boko Haram began as a religious educational group with radical ideas for change. The source of many of its extreme views stems from its close ties to the **Salafi** Islamic religious circle, or Wahhabites.

Wahhabism is a revivalist movement founded in the Arabian Peninsula in 1744. It was named for its founder, Muhammad ibn Abd al-Wahhab. He urged a return to a pure, **unadulterated** form of Islam, closer to the ideals of the Prophet Muhammad. Wahhabism falls under the umbrella of a school of medieval Islam known as **Salafiyyah**. Early followers of the school—**Salifis**—believed they could reconcile Islam with modern Western political thought. Later Islamic reformers branded modern Western culture as barbaric and called for a doctrine of jihad—"holy war"—to liberate the entire world so that only Islam would prevail. Boko Haram embraced the latter thinking.

CHAPTER 2

"The formation of this group and many others can be traced to [the] unbridled growth of religious fanaticism due to poverty and growing unemployment in Nigeria and West African states from the late 1980s," writes counterterrorism expert Don Michael Adeniji. "Religious renaissance in youths with identity problem[s] blossomed in religious circle[s] as many thronged to religion in search of hope as economic recession hit hard and poverty increased."[2] Government corruption and mismanagement that gave preferential treatment to southern Nigerians, along with the brutally harsh crackdown by Nigeria's security apparatus, added fuel to the rebellious fires in the bellies of northern Nigerian youths. According to Nigerian political activist Osita Ebiem, who advocates a multi-state solution to his country's problems,

> Boko Haram is a fundamentalist jihadist group, which believes that Western education and civilization are corrupting the Muslims of Nigeria and they are on a mission to purify the religion and create an Islamic country in Northern Nigeria. They want to build a society—a separate political state in Northern Nigeria that is ruled by **Sharia** and free from all corrupting agents such as Christians and all institutions that represent Christianity.[3]

Boko Haram leadership did not call for violence during its formative years. From the early 2000s to 2009, its followers engaged in periodic, low-level conflict with local police forces as well as with dissenting villagers.

In July 2009, police in Borno state cracked down on Boko Haram members and fighting erupted. At least 700 people were killed during an effort by Nigerian security forces to suppress the group. Savage clashes spread across the three northern Nigerian states of Bauchi, Kano, and Yobe, as Boko Haram turned to violence.

Terrorism

Mayhem in Maiduguri

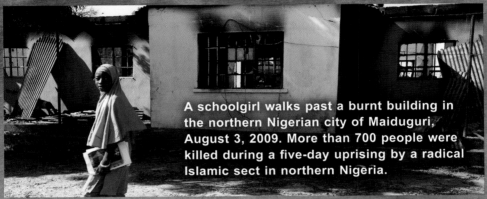

A schoolgirl walks past a burnt building in the northern Nigerian city of Maiduguri, August 3, 2009. More than 700 people were killed during a five-day uprising by a radical Islamic sect in northern Nigeria.

The Boko Haram uprising of 2009 ended in a fight in Maiduguri, the capital of Borno state. Fighting erupted when a group of Boko Haram were en route to a cemetery for the burial service of one of their members. Police stopped them and ordered them to obey a law that required passengers in motorcycles to wear helmets. The young men refused to obey the order. In the heated argument that followed, police shot and wounded several of them.

Sect leader Mohammed Yusuf retaliated by ordering attacks on police stations and government buildings. Soon afterward, Nigerian Army troops assaulted Yusuf's compound. They also stormed a nearby mosque where his followers had barricaded themselves. Nigerian Security Forces (NSF) fighters killed many Boko Haram and forced others to flee. Army and police forces also engaged militants in house-to-house fighting. The fighting in Maiduguri claimed the lives of more than 700 people, including an unreported number of Nigerian policemen.

NSF officers captured Yusuf and later shot him dead while in custody, allegedly while he was trying to escape. A British newsman was shown a film of what appeared to be Yusuf's body, riddled with bullets and stone-cold dead while still wearing handcuffs. He probably wasn't the only one. According to numerous media reports, other militants were executed by the police.

But out of the bloody mayhem that was Maiduguri, a new Boko Haram leader emerged—Abubakar Shekau.

Nigerian president Goodluck Jonathan is shown after he delivered an address at the World Economic Forum in Davos, Switzerland. The theme of the annual meeting, held on January 23, 2013, was "De-risking Africa—Achieving Inclusive Prosperity."

CHAPTER 3
Waging War on Infidels

After the shoot-out at Maiduguri, the government banned Boko Haram. Its members went underground for a year to regroup. Before his death while in the custody of Nigerian security forces, Yusuf had organized the sect in a hierarchical or pyramidal structure—that is, a top-down ranking of leaders and subordinates.

Yusuf appointed himself as Commander-in-Chief and Spiritual Leader (Amir ul-Aam) of the faithful. A First and Second Deputy below him reported directly to him. The three of them formed part of the Shura Consultative Council at the next level downward. The Shura (council) serves as the sect's legislative organ. It controls the activities of the State Operational Commanders and Strategists at the next lower level. Below them, Local Cell Operational Commanders and Strategists direct the affairs of the Operational Cells that form the base of the pyramidal structure.[1]

In July 2010, Abubakar Shekau, who had been second-in-command of Boko Haram under Yusuf, released a video identifying himself as the new leader. In the video, he also praised two fallen leaders of al-Qaeda in Iraq (AQI): "By Allah, they rose, did jihad, and fought in order for the faith to be entirely for Allah. It was for this that they fought, and it was for this that they died." He called them both "martyrs" and went on to warn: "Do not think that jihad is over. Rather jihad has just begun. O America, die with your fury."[2]

Shekau offered support and pledged allegiance to the Afghani Taliban and al-Qaeda Central (or Core al-Qaeda). At the same time, however, he conceded that Boko Haram did not currently maintain ties with either group. Direct evidence tying the group to al-Qaeda remains elusive. Many analysts assert that a link between them does in fact exist, however, if only in funding from al-Qaeda thought to be received by Boko Haram.

Shekau's admonition to America in that same statement served notice of his intention to expand Boko Haram's operations beyond local boundaries and introduce an international reach. It also revealed an early indication that Shekau was a different breed of animal than his predecessor, Mohammed Yusuf.

Yusuf, a **charismatic** preacher, had built his reputation lecturing against Western education. He consistently condemned the existing system in Nigeria and advocated the overthrow of the government. In its place, he and his followers wanted to install an Islamic state in the north with strict adherence to Sharia law. He originally tried to achieve this goal non-violently.

Shekau, by contrast, immediately focused on jihad. Under his leadership, Boko Haram became a *takfiri* organization, one that accused dissenting Muslim groups as being **apostates** (unbelievers or **infidels**). He publicly criticized Yusuf before his death for being too soft, and signaled his intentions to lead in a different direction. Experts cite one of his early video appearances as a possible window into his character. "I enjoy killing anyone that God commands me to kill," he boasted after carrying out an attack that claimed 180 lives. "The way I enjoy killing chickens and rams."[3]

Under Shekau's leadership, Boko Haram resurfaced a year after the defeat at Maiduguri with attacks on police stations and military barracks, seeking revenge for the killings of Yusuf and other comrades. They conducted jailbreaks to free imprisoned members and demanded the prosecution of Yusuf's killers. They further pressed for compensation for members killed by troops and restoration of the mosque that had been destroyed in the earlier fighting.

Though Boko Haram originally targeted security forces and government officials, Shekau expanded its operations to include attacks on Christians, traditional leaders, suspected collaborators, U.N. agencies, and bars. Their evolving terrorist activities extended to assaults on students at state (**secular**) schools and health workers administering polio vaccinations. They soon progressed to assassinating neighborhood chiefs suspected of identifying their members to the military and Muslim clerics who spoke out against their **ideology**.

On Christmas Eve 2010, Boko Haram claimed responsibility for multiple bomb attacks on churches and other targets in several central Nigerian cities. Nearly 40 people died, sparking violent reprisals that killed at least another 80 people. A statement on the Boko Haram website attributed to Abubakar Shekau noted: "My message to my Muslim brethren is that they should know that this is a war between Muslims and infidels. This is a religious war."[4] It marked their first attack outside northern Nigeria.

The year 2011 proved to be eventful for Nigeria, filled with social upheaval and political developments. Most Nigerians turned out for elections in April. To the displeasure of most Muslims, Goodluck Jonathan, a Christian, was elected president. The following month, an ethnic conflict broke out in the state and city of Jos. Many Muslims were brutalized. Adding to the carnage, Boko Haram attacked Christians in churches in retaliation. Nigerian records list several other major Boko Haram operations in 2011. One came on June 16 and involved a targeted bomb attack. A car bomber blew himself up in a failed attempt to kill the head of the Nigerian police. The blast left at least six people dead in Nigeria's first-ever suicide bombing. On August 26, a second bombing attack toppled part of the United Nations building in Abuja, killing 25 people and injuring more than a hundred others. On Christmas Day, churches in several cities provided the targets for Boko Haram bombings that killed at least 40 people and injured many more. In all, more than 550 people lost their lives in 2011 in more than 100 attacks.

On the day after the bombing of the U.N. headquarters, President Jonathan stood in front of the still-smoldering rubble and said, "Boko Haram is a local group linked up with terrorist activities, and as a government we are working on it and we will bring it under control."[5] Jonathan wasn't much of a prophet. In 2012, Boko Haram escalated its terrorist activities exponentially.

In the aftermath of a bombing at St. Theresa Catholic Church on Christmas Day, 2011, in the Nigerian town of Madalla, just outside the capital Abuja, smoke and flames still pour out of a wrecked car in an impromptu graveyard of bombed-out vehicles. Boko Haram claimed responsibility for five bombings at churches in Nigeria that day, leaving 27 dead in an effort to incite a sectarian civil war.

Abubakar Shekau

Boko Haram leader Abubakar Shekau, with an AK-47, speaks to the camera in this image taken from a video on May 12, 2014.

Abubakar Shekau, also known as Abu Muhammad Abubakar bin Muhammad, is a man shrouded in mystery and unknowns. Some say he was born in the Republic of Niger; others note his birth in Yobe state in Nigeria. Estimates of his birthdate range from 1965 to 1975. He was reported dead on several occasions, but each time he soon reappeared to escalate his campaign of terror against infidels and authority figures. When the U.S. government placed a bounty of $7 million on his head in 2013, he became one of the most wanted men in the world.

Shekau is a Muslim theologian, an intellectual, and a cold-blooded killer. In 1990, he moved to Maiduguri, where he met Mohammed Yusuf about a decade later. He became his second-in-command in Boko Haram and ultimate successor.

Shekau's leadership philosophy is simple and chilling: "It is Allah that instructed us," he once said in labored English. "Until we soak the ground of Nigeria with Christian blood and so-called Muslims contradicting Islam. After we have killed, killed, killed, and get fatigue and wondering what to do with their corpses—smelling of [Barack] Obama, [George] Bush and [Goodluck] Jonathan—will open prison and be imprison the rest. Infidels have no value."[6]

On September 7, 2010, Boko Haram launched a surprise attack at sunset on a prison in Bauchi, Nigeria, to free more than a hundred of their fellow militants. Armed with assault rifles and explosives, they mounted a highly coordinated assault that left the prison in ruins, here examined by an unidentified official. The attack occurred only months before scheduled elections. It revealed Boko Haram's access to sophisticated weaponry and raised fears of renewed violence in the oil-rich nation.

CHAPTER 4
Caught Between Two Evils

On New Year's Eve 2011, President Jonathan declared a state of emergency in parts of the northeastern Borno and Yobe states, as well as in the central Plateau and Niger states. He also established a special force unit within the Nigerian Armed Forces, dedicated to counterterrorism duties. The president's new crackdown on terrorism ushered in a new surge of violence.

Boko Haram wrote new stories in blood in 2012. They carried out their first horrific tale of note in the New Year in the northern city of Kano on January 20. Using car bombs, suicide bombers, and improvised explosive devices (IEDs), waves of gunmen set upon the state and regional police headquarters, three local police stations, and a police barracks. They also struck the offices of the State Security Service (SSS) and the immigration department. Officially, 185 people—mostly civilians—died in the attack that day. Kano residents put the death toll much higher.

Despite the carnage, some residents so despised the authorities in Kano—who were feared as much as the terrorists for their brutal enforcement of the law—they actually cheered on the attackers. Ken Saro-Wiwa, a Kano resident, summed up the peoples' impressions of the attack in telling terms to *National Geographic* journalist James Verini. "To live a day in Nigeria is to die many times,"[1] he said.

The use of car bombs, suicide bombers, and IEDs by Boko Haram lent **credence** to contentions of their growing affiliation with "core" al-Qaeda-linked terror groups. As early as January 2010, Abdelmalek Droukdel, the leader of al-Qaeda in the Islamic **Maghreb** (AQIM), announced that AQIM would help Boko

Haram with training, personnel, and equipment. The Maghreb originally consisted of the Arab-speaking countries of northwest Africa—Morocco, Algeria, and Tunisia. After the 1970s, it was extended to include Mauritania and part of Libya.

The previous November, Abu Qaqa, Boko Haram's official spokesman, confirmed its connection with al-Qaeda. "We are together with al-Qaeda," he declared. "They are promoting the cause of Islam just as we are doing. Therefore they help us in our struggle and we help them, too."[2]

Reportedly, Boko Haram's connection to al-Qaeda-linked groups extends beyond AQIM. Some members are known to have received training from the Somali terrorist group al-Shabaab in East Africa. Other members have been tied to the Yemen-based al-Qaeda in the Arabian Peninsula (AQAP).

On February 20, 2012, striking in the town where they had originated, Boko Haram gunmen stormed the Baga market in Maiduguri. They began firing indiscriminately and setting off bombs. Boko Haram claimed that merchants had collaborated with the military after the arrest of one of its members. Members of the Joint Task Force (JTF) at the market responded to the attack and a firefight ensued. The incident claimed the lives of eight assailants and at least 30 others, including women and children. An eyewitness later reported seeing three military vans piled with bodies. On Easter Sunday, a suicide car bomb exploded outside the All Nations Christian Assembly Church in Kaduna in central Nigeria. The explosion killed 40 people. No one claimed responsibility, but the blast bore the mark of Boko Haram.

On July 7, Boko Haram operatives mounted six coordinated attacks in six villages across volatile Plateau state, killing at least 65 people. Two months later, Boko Haram attacked 31 cell towers with explosives in coordinated attacks across four states, supposedly because cell companies had assisted the government in its counterterrorism efforts. About 15 people died in the blasts. The next day, in six more coordinated attacks, Boko Haram militants attacked two government buildings, two schools, a fire station, and an electoral office. About 15 people were killed.

Continuing their coordinated attacks on October 18, Boko Haram members struck an Islamic seminary school and two primary schools in the northeastern city of Potiskum, killing 23 people. Boko Haram closed out the year with two more coordinated attacks in the city of Jaji in north-central Nigeria on November 25. Group members drove an explosive-laden bus into St. Andrew Military Protestant Church. They followed the blast with a car-bomb attack on first responders. The two blasts combined to claim 32 lives and wound 11 other people.

By the end of 2012, nearly 800 people had been killed as Boko Haram showed no signs of stopping or reducing its violent attacks. Making things worse, to the distress of everyday Nigerians, government forces were compiling a long list of human rights abuses against its citizens in their zeal to combat Boko Haram and other terrorists. A U.S. Department of State report in 2012 documented some of the security breaches:

> [H]uman rights problems included extrajudicial [without legal authority] killings by security forces, including summary executions; security force torture, rape, and other cruel, inhuman, or degrading treatment of prisoners, detainees, and criminal suspects; harsh and life-threatening prison and detention center conditions; arbitrary arrest and detention; prolonged pretrial detention; denial of fair public trial . . .[3]

The list went on. And Nigerians suffered the consequences of being caught in the middle of two forces bent on violence and destruction.

"Of the more than 4,700 killings associated with Boko Haram to date, almost half have been at the hands of security forces,

Government forces announced that two Boko Haram fighters were killed and two others wounded when a bomb exploded in the Gandu neighborhood of Kano on March 24, 2012. The explosion occurred during a raid on a suspected terrorist hideout. Wives and children of the sect members sit outside the hideout after the raid.

according to Human Rights Watch," wrote journalist James Verini in 2013. "Many of those killed have been civilians who were just in the wrong place at the wrong time. As the insurgency gets more vicious, so does the government."[4]

The cycle of killing continued in 2013. Boko Haram's first large-scale effort that year occurred on May 7 in a series of coordinated attacks in Bama town in Borno state. Some 200 heavily armed men stormed a military barracks, a police station, and several government buildings. They struck with armored vehicles fitted with machine guns. Boko Haram had now gone mechanized. The raiders killed 55 people and freed 105 prisoners. A week later, President Jonathan declared another state of emergency in the three northern states of Yobe, Borno, and Adamawa, which were Boko Haram strongholds.

A House Divided

During the five years of Abubakar Shekau's reign as leader of Boko Haram, differences about the group's targets and geographical areas of operations often cropped up. Some commanders vigorously opposed Shekau's leadership. Among them was Mamman Nur, a Cameroon citizen who had been third-in-command of Boko Haram under Yusuf and Shekau.

During the 2009 clash in which Yusuf was slain, Shekau had been wounded and temporarily detained. Nur became interim leader of the group until Shekau's release. Some militants felt that Nur was a more competent leader than Shekau. Among other things, Nur took issue with Shekau's policy of killing fellow Muslims who disagreed with him.

On January 26, 2012, a spinoff group calling itself Ansaru released flyers in Kano publicly announcing its formation. Ansaru claimed to be a humane alternative to Boko Haram and vowed to target only Nigerian government officials and Christians in self-defense. The new group identified its leader as Abu Usmatul al-Ansari, believed to be an alias for Mamman Nur. Ansaru openly declared its intent to target Western nationals beyond Nigeria's borders. Meanwhile, Boko Haram continued to spill blood and spread terror as a house divided.

Newspaper headlines on March 10, 2013 proclaim the killings of seven foreign hostages by the Nigerian extremist group calling itself Ansaru.

Fugitives from Boko Haram terrorist acts occasionally fled from Nigeria to Chad. Aisha al-Haji Garba, from the Nigerian town of Doron Baga, cradles her baby at a refugee camp in Baga Sola, Chad. Aisha struggled across Lake Chad on her dangerous journey while pregnant. She gave birth shortly after arriving in Chad.

CHAPTER 5
Targeting Westerners

The U.S. Department of State designated Boko Haram and its splinter group Ansaru as Foreign Terror Organizations (FTOs) in November 2013. Given the murderous track records of the two groups, some observers might wonder what took State so long.

Testimony offered before Congress by Nigerian human rights activist Emmanuel Ogebe on September 18, 2014, serves as a case in point. "Boko Haram has claimed the lives of over 10,000 people since 2009, both Nigerian nationals and international victims," he noted. "They have killed individuals from over 15 nations—far more than ISIS, al-Qaeda, and possibly the Taliban."[1] Boko Haram's killing machine remained on a fast track to reach its **zenith** in 2014.

On February 15, nearly a hundred Boko Haram terrorists roared into the Christian farming village of Izghe on trucks and motorcycles. Quickly overwhelming the villagers, the militants opened fire on residents gathered in the town square and hacked the males to death. Not yet done with their mission to eradicate Christians, the raiders went house to house, door to door, shooting or slitting the throats of their victims. Numbered among their victims was a grandmother who tried to save the life of her grandson. In their wake, they left 106 residents dead.

The Izghe massacre followed on the heels of an earlier attack that morning on Doron Baga, a fishing village on Lake Chad. Babagana Gwoni, a survivor of the attack, told CNN: "They opened fire from all directions, forcing residents to jump into the lake in a bid to escape, and many drowned while others were gunned down."[2] Before leaving, the gunmen ransacked the town's fish and food supplies and torched the homes.

Nine days later, Boko Haram raiders struck again. In a pre-dawn attack on a boarding school in Buni Yadi, the Islamic militants slaughtered 59 boys. Sparing female students in the attack, the attackers moved to a dormitory where males were sleeping, locked the door, and set the dorm ablaze. As the trapped boys tried to escape, the raiders slit their throats and gunned down those who tried to run away. They burned down the school before leaving.

The burned-out remains of Federal Government College in Buni Tadi, Nigeria. On February 25, 2014, Boko Haram terrorists launched a predawn attack on the northeast Nigerian school. The attackers locked the dormitory, set it aflame, and shot and slit the throats of dozens of students as they tried to escape through windows. Surviving witnesses reported that many victims were burned alive.

Meanwhile, Boko Haram's splinter group Ansaru—even before publicly identifying itself—had introduced the kidnapping of foreign nationals as a new weapon in the arsenal of Nigerian terrorists. In May 2011, they abducted an Italian and a Briton in northwest Nigeria. Almost a year later, they took both captives to a toilet and shot them dead during a failed rescue attempt by a joint British and Nigerian force.

In 2011, Nigeria had begun to deploy security forces in counterterrorism operations with marginal success. A State Department report in 2013 listed some of the factors limiting the Nigerian government's response to the growing threat posed by Boko Haram and its affiliates. They included a lack of coordination and cooperation between Nigerian security agencies, corruption, misuse of resources, inadequate databases, the slow-working judicial system, and ill-trained prosecutors and judges to implement anti-terrorism laws. Consequently, the morale of Nigerian troops declined so much that they grew fearful and afraid to even engage the terrorists.

Traditionally, U.S. policy toward a terrorist group has been determined by the extent to which it poses a direct threat to the United States and its interests. Until recently, U.S. policymakers ranked al-Shabaab in Somalia as the primary terrorist threat in Africa. In light of Boko Haram's growing menace, that ranking may be shifting.

In early 2014, U.S. Director of National Intelligence James Clapper outlined various threats facing the nation. They included "critical terrorism threats from Boko Haram and persistent extremism in the north, simmering ethno-religious conflict . . . and militants who are capable of remobilizing in the Niger Delta and attacking the oil industry." Clapper went on to warn about "rising political tensions and violent internal conflict" in the lead-up to Nigeria's 2015 election. He cautioned that "protests and

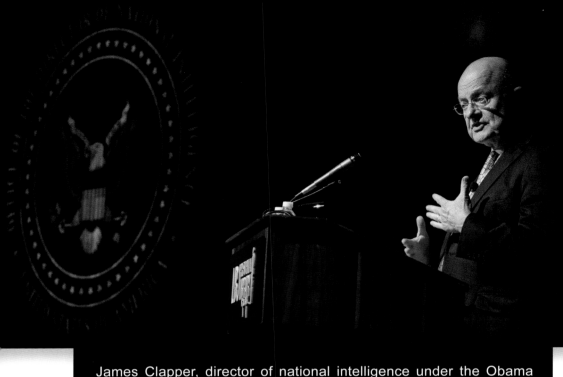

James Clapper, director of national intelligence under the Obama administration, warned that Boko Haram represented a critical threat to inciting an ethno-religious conflict in northern Nigeria and to potentially attacking the nation's oil industry in the south.

upheaval, especially in northern Nigeria, are likely in the event of President Goodluck Jonathan's reelection."[3]

Critics accused Jonathan—a Christian from prosperous southern Nigeria—of indifference toward the plight of poor northern Nigerians, particularly Muslims. Other detractors contended that he was incompetent and unable to guarantee the safety of Nigerians. During the kidnapping of the Chibok schoolgirls, he earned further disfavor by criticizing the parents of the girls for not cooperating with the police or sharing information.

Nigeria's First Lady, Patience Jonathan, added to the popular resentment of her husband's administration with a public display of insensitivity. During the Chibok kidnapping incident, as reported by Nicole Lee from the TransAfrica Forum, she "called some of the mothers to her, to meet with her, and she basically told them that they really needed to be quiet and they were really bringing shame and embarrassment to Nigeria. That's certainly a problem."[4] Her callous remarks were not likely to enhance the campaign of a politician running for reelection.

As Nigerians looked ahead for solutions to their problems, the United States was paying close attention to the escalating terrorist activities of Boko Haram. In a 2013 report, the State Department stated that "of particular concern to the United States is the emergence of the BH [Boko Haram] faction known as 'Ansaru,' which has close ties to AQIM and has prioritized targeting Westerners—including Americans—in Nigeria."[5]

The report went on to acknowledge that the threat was growing, further noting that "elements of BH increased the number and sophistication of attacks . . . with a notable increase in the lethality, capability, and coordination of attacks."[6] The efforts of Jonathan and his administration to combat Boko Haram proved insufficient and ineffective.

Nigerians had reason for hope on October 17, 2014 when the government announced a cease-fire agreement with Boko Haram. Supposedly the remaining Chibok girls would be released. It was illusory. Attacks within 24 hours of the announcement made it clear that Boko Haram had no intention of stopping its terrorist activities, both inside Nigeria and beyond. It further increased its lethality by declaring its allegiance to the self-declared Islamic State (IS) in March 2015. Its elimination would require joint efforts to enhance the capability of Nigerian security forces and military, restore trust in Nigeria's government among much of its population, and provide workable solutions to the long-term problems of its citizens—particularly those in the north. To that end, Nigerians elected a new president, Muhammadu Buhari, in May 2015. Buhari vowed to end the Boko Haram insurgency within months.

In Abuja, President Muhammadu Buhari, dressed in black and smiling, along with Vice President Yemi Osinbajo, stages a reception for 21 Chibok schoolgirls released by Boko Haram on October 19, 2016. But many girls remain captives of the terrorists.

Terrorism

Dying Hard

In August 2016, the Islamic State militant group announced in its online magazine that Boko Haram had a new leader, Abu Musab al-Barnawi. It did not indicate what had happened to Shekau. Despite the war being waged against it by President Buhari's government forces, Barnawi said Boko Haram continued to draw new recruits and "remained a force to be reckoned with."[7]

Two months later, a spokesperson for Buhari announced that 21 of the Chibok schoolgirls had been freed after negotiations with Boko Haram. Local sources indicated they had been exchanged for four Boko Haram prisoners. More than 200 of the kidnapped girls remain missing, but the release of some of the girls bodes well for the eventual recovery of the rest.

On December 24, 2016, President Buhari declared that his forces had crushed Boko Haram and driven them from their last hideout in the Sambisa Forest. But three days after Buhari claimed victory, his media and publicity aide Femi Adesina cautioned, "Even as Sambisa Forest has been taken over, you will still find some elements who will continue to fight and they will be taken out eventually. This kind of war is not one that at a point you will say because Sambisa has been taken over, it's over for now, no! It is over when we stop having strikes and attacks."[8]

Estimates of those killed by Boko Haram militants during their multi-year insurgency range from 17,000 to more than 30,000 victims. Today, Boko Haram remains alive, active, and dangerous—and it will likely die hard.

2002 Boko Haram founded by Mohammed Yusuf in Maiduguri, Nigeria.

2009 Boko Haram uprising ends with the killing of Mohammed Yusuf in Maiduguri on July 30.

2010

July Abubakar Shekau declares himself leader of Boko Haram in a video.

December 24 Boko Haram claims responsibility for multiple bombings.

2011

April 18 Goodluck Jonathan is elected President of Nigeria.

June 16 A Boko Haram suicide-bomber fails in an attempt to kill the head of the Nigerian police.

August 26 Boko Haram terrorists bomb UN building in Abuja.

December 25 Boko Haram bombs churches in several cities.

December 31 President Jonathan declares a state of emergency in several states.

2012

January 20 Waves of Boko Haram gunmen attack the northern city of Kano.

January 26 Ansaru publicly announces its formation.

February 20 Boko Haram gunmen storm Baga market in Maiduguri.

March 8 Ansaru terrorists kill Western hostages abducted in May 2011.

April 8 Car bomb kills 40 at a Christian church in Kaduna.

July 7 Boko Haram operatives mount six coordinated attacks across Plateau state.

October 18 Boko Haram members strike schools in Potiskum.

November 25 Boko Haram bombers strike Christian church in Jaji.

2013

May 7 Boko Haram raiders attack government facilities in Bama town in Borno state.

May 14 President Jonathan declares another state of emergency in the northern states of Yobe, Borno, and Adamawa.

2014

February 15 Boko Haram terrorists mount massive raids on the villages of Izghe and Doron Baga.

February 24 Boko Haram raiders slaughter 59 boys at a school in Buni Yadi.

April 14–15 Boko Haram militants kidnap schoolgirls in Chibok.

May 5 Boko Haram leader Abubakar Chekau claims responsibility for kidnapping Chibok schoolgirls.

May 11 Nigerian President Jonathan pledges to rescue Chibok schoolgirls.

October 17 Nigerian military announces a cease-fire agreement with Boko Haram.

2015

March 7 Boko Haram pledges allegiance to the Islamic State (IS).

May 29 Nigeria swears in new President Muhammadu Buhari.

2016

April 13 Tearful Nigerian mothers recognize their daughters on Boko Haram video.

August 3 Islamic State announces Abu Musab al-Barnawi as new leader of Boko Haram.

October 13 Spokesperson for President Buhari confirms the release of 21 Chibok girls.

December 24 Nigerian president Buhari declares that Boko Haram has been crushed and driven from its last forest stronghold.

2017

May 6 82 more Chibok girls are released in exchange for a number of Boko Haram suspects held by the government.

CHAPTER NOTES

Chapter 1   Lives at Risk

1. David Smith and Harriet Sherwood, "Military operation launched to locate kidnapped Nigerian girls." *The Guardian*, May 14, 2014. http://www.theguardian.com/world/2014/may/14/nigeria-launches-military-operation-to-find-kidnapped-girls

2. Adam Nossiter, "Tales of Escapees in Nigeria Add to Worries About Other Kidnapped Girls." *The New York Times*, May 14, 2014. http://www.nytimes.com/2014/05/15/world/africa/tales-of-escapees-in-nigeria-add-to-worries-about-other-kidnapped-girls.html?_r=0

3. Ibid.

4. Ibid.

5. Ibid.

6. Ibid.

7. Ibid.

8. Aminu Abubakar and Josh Levs, "'I will sell them,' Boko Haram leader says of kidnapped Nigerian girls." CNN, May 6, 2014. http://www.cnn.com/2014/05/05/world/africa/nigeria-abducted-girls/?hpt=bosread

9. Alex Moe, "Hillary Clinton: Kidnappings in Nigeria Are 'Abominable.'" NBC News, May 7, 2014. http://www.nbcnews.com/storyline/missing-nigeria-schoolgirls/hillary-clinton-kidnappings-nigeria-are-abominable-n99721

10. Darlene Superville, "Michelle Obama speaks out on kidnapped Nigerian schoolgirls." Associated Press, May 10, 2014. http://www.pbs.org/newshour/rundown/flotus-speaks-kidnapped-nigerian-girls/

11. Smith and Sherwood, "Military operation."

12. Abubakar and Levs, "'I will sell them.'"

13. Moe, "Hillary Clinton."

14. Michael Martinez, Pierre Meilhan, and Faith Karimi, "'War on Boko Haram': African, Western nations unify in hunt for Nigerian girls." CNN, May 17, 2014. http://edition.cnn.com/2014/05/17/world/africa/nigeria-abducted-girls/

Chapter 2   Turning to Violence

1. Richard Simons, *Not with Our Daughters: Boko Haram & the Kidnapping of 300 Nigerian Schoolgirls: A New Pattern of Terror the World Must Unite and Stop* (Charleston, SC: CreateSpace Publishing, 2014), p. 61.

2. Don Michael Adeniji, *Boko Haram: Designing Effective Counter-Terrorism Programme* (Raleigh, NC: Lulu Press, 2014), p. 170.

3. Osita Ebiem, *Nigeria, Biafra and Boko Haram: Ending the Genocides Through Multistate Solution* (New York: Page Publishing, 2014), p. 113.

Chapter 3   Waging War on Infidels

1. Don Michael Adeniji, *Boko Haram: Designing Effective Counter-Terrorism Programme* (Raleigh, NC: Lulu Press, 2014), pp. 186-87.

2. Joseph Joscelyn, "A Well-Deserved Terrorist Designation." *The Weekly Standard*. November 13, 2013. http://www.weeklystandard.com/print/blogs/well-deserved-terrorist-designation_767037.html

3. Terrence McCoy, "The man behind the Nigerian girls' kidnappings and his death-defying mystique." *The Washington Post,* May 6, 2014. http://www.washingtonpost.com/news/morning-mix/wp/2014/05/06/the-man-behind-the-nigerian-girls-kidnappings-and-his-death-defying-mystique/?tid=hp_mm&hpid=z3

4. "Muslim group claims Nigeria blasts." *Aljazeera,* December 28, 2010. http://www.aljazeera.com/news/africa/2010/12/20101228123525363633.html

5. Christopher Bartolotta, "Terrorism in Nigeria: the Rise of Boko Haram." http://www.worldpolicy.org/blog/2011/09/19/terrorism-nigeria-rise-boko-haram

6. McCoy, "The man behind the Nigerian girls' kidnappings."

Chapter 4   Caught Between Two Evils

1. James Verini, "The War for Nigeria." *National Geographic*, November 2013, p. 105.

2. U.S. House of Representatives Committee on Homeland Security, *Boko Haram: Growing Threat to U.S. Homeland* (Charleston, SC: CreateSpace Publishing, 2014), p. 20.

3. U.S. Department of State, Bureau of Democracy, Human Rights and Labor. "Country Reports on Human Rights Practices for 2012: Nigeria." http://www.state.gov/j/drl/rls/hrrpt/humanrightsreport/index.htm?year=2012&dlid=204153

4. Verini, "The War for Nigeria," p. 107.

Chapter 5   Targeting Westerners

1. Emmanuel Ogebe, "More deadly than ISIS and al-Qaeda." World News Group, September 27, 2014. http://www.worldmag.com/2014/09/more_deadly_than_isis_and_al_qaeda/

2. Morgan Lee, "Islamic Militants Hack to Death, Brutally Murder 106 Residents of Christian Farming Village in Nigeria." *The Christian Post*, February 18, 2014. http://m.christianpost.com/news/islamic-militants-hack-to-death-brutally-murder-106-residents-of-christian-farming-village-in-nigeria-114692/

3. Lauren Ploch Blanchard, "Nigeria's Boko Haram: Frequently Asked Questions." Congressional Research Service. June 10, 2014. http://fas.org/sgp/crs/row/R43558.pdf

4. Holly Yan, "Nigeria abductions: 6 reasons why the world should demand action." CNN. May 6, 2014. http://www.cnn.com/2014/05/06/world/africa/nigeria-abductions-why-it-matters/

5. U.S. House of Representatives Committee on Homeland Security. *Boko Haram: Growing Threat to U.S. Homeland* (Charleston, SC: CreateSpace Publishing, 2014), p. 38.

6. Ibid.

7. "Boko Haram in Nigeria: Abu Musab al-Barnawi named as new leader." BBC News, August 3, 2016. http://www.bbc.com/news/world-africa-36963711

8. Mandy Oteng, "Buhari never said that war against Boko Haram is over—Adesina." Online Nigeria, December 27, 2016. http://news2.onlinenigeria.com/news/general/579587-buhari-never-said-that-war-against-boko-haram-is-over-adesina.html

Femi Adesina (FEH-mee ah-dee-SEE-nuh)—Media and publicity aide to current president of Nigeria Muhammadu Buhari.

Abu Usmatal al-Ansari (AH-boo ooz-MAT-ahl AHN-suh-ree)—Alias of Mamman Nur.

Abu Musab al-Barnawi (AH-boo moo-SAHB ahl-bar-NAH-we)—Current leader of Boko Haram.

Muhammadu Buhari (moo-HAH-mah-dew bu-HAH-ree)—Current president of Nigeria.

David Cameron—Prime Minister of Great Britain.

James Clapper—Director of U.S. National Intelligence.

Hillary Clinton—Former First Lady of the United States, senator, and secretary of state.

Abdelmalek Droukdel (ab-del-MAHL-ek DROWK-del)—Leader of al-Qaeda in the Islamic Maghreb (AQIM).

François Hollande (frahn-SWAH oh-LAHN-deh)—President of France.

Goodluck Jonathan—Former president of Nigeria.

Patience Jonathan—Former First Lady of Nigeria.

Mamman Nur (MAM-man NOOR)—Leader of Ansaru.

Barack Obama—Forty-fourth President of the United States.

Michelle Obama—Former First Lady of the United States.

Abu Qaqa (AH-boo KUH-kuh)—Official spokesman for Boko Haram.

Abubakar Shekau (ah-boo-BAH-kar she-KAW)—Former leader of the Nigerian militant group Boko Haram.

Muhammad ibn Abd al-Wahhab (moo-HAH-mahd ib-uhn ab-dahl-wa-HAHB)—Founder of Wahhabism in the Arabian Peninsula in 1744.

Mohammed Yusuf (moh-HAH-mehd YOO-sehf)—Founder and first leader of Boko Haram.

GLOSSARY

apostate (uh-POS-tayt)—one who renounces a religious faith

camos (CAM-ohz)—short for camouflage clothing

charismatic (cair-uz-MAT-ik)– exceptional degree of charm that inspires loyalty and devotion from others

coerce (coe-ERSS)—obtain something by using force or the threat of force

credence (CREE-dunce)—believing that something is true

ideology (ih-dee-AHL-oh-jee)—the principal ideas or beliefs that characterize a particular, class, group, or movement

infidels (IN-fuh-dehls)—people who don't believe in a particular religion

Islam (IS-lahm, or is-LAHM)—the Muslim religion, based on the teachings of Muhammad; the Muslim world

Maghreb (MUH-greb)—countries of northwest Africa: Morocco, Algeria, Tunisia, Mauritania, and part of Libya

philanthropic (fil-an-THROP-ik)—benevolent; concerned with human welfare and the reduction of suffering

primeval (pry-MEE-vuhl)—the earliest ages in world history

profane (proh-FANE)—disrespectful of religious practice

propagation (praw-puh-GAY-shun)—widely spreading an idea

protectorate (proh-TEK-toh-rit)—a weak or underdeveloped country under the official protection and partial control of a stronger one

Quran (kuh-RAN)—Book composed of sacred writings accepted by Muslims as revelations made to Muhammad by Allah through the angel Gabriel

revelatory (REH-vuhl-uh-tor-ee)—making something known

Salafiyyah (sal-uh-FIGH-yuh)—way of the ancestors; medieval school of Islam.

Salifi (suh-LIHF-ee)—militant group of extremist Muslims who believe themselves the only correct interpreters of the Quran and consider moderate Muslims to be infidels

Sambisa Forest (sam-BEEZ-uh FOR-ist)—game reserve in northeastern Nigeria

secular (SEK-yew-lahr)—concerned with worldly affairs rather than spiritual ones.

Sharia (shah-REE-uh)—Islamic law

takfir (tak-FEAR)—to accuse another of disbelief and infidelity.

unadulterated (uhn-uh-DUHL-ter-a-ted)—complete, not mixed with anything else

Wahhabism (wah-HAH-bi-zem)—an Islamic revivalist movement founded in the Arabian Peninsula in 1744.

zenith (ZEE-nith)—highest point

FURTHER READING

Bedell, J. M. *Combatting Terrorism*. North Mankato, MN: Compass Point Books, 2010.

Friedman, Lauri. *Terrorist Attacks*. San Diego: ReferencePoint Press, 2008.

Nardo, Don. *The History of Terrorism*. North Mankato, MN: Compass Point Books, 2010.

Netzley, Patricia D. *Terrorism and the War of the 2000s*. San Diego: ReferencePoint Press, 2014.

Ruschmann, Paul. *The War on Terror*. 2d ed. New York: Chelsea House, 2008.

WORKS CONSULTED

Abubakar, Aminu, and Josh Levs. "'I will sell them,' Boko Haram leader says of kidnapped Nigerian girls." CNN, May 6, 2014. http://www.cnn.com/2014/05/05/world/africa/nigeria-abducted-girls/?hpt=bosread

Adeniji, Don Michael. *Boko Haram: Designing Effective Counter-Terrorism Programme*. Raleigh, NC: Lulu Press, 2014.

Bartolotta, Christopher. "Terrorism in Nigeria: the Rise of Boko Haram." http://www.worldpolicy.org/blog/2011/09/19/terrorism-nigeria-rise-boko-haram

Blanchard, Lauren Ploch. "Nigeria's Boko Haram: Frequently Asked Questions." Congressional Research Service. June 10, 2014. http://fas.org/sgp/crs/row/R43558.pdf

"Boko Haram in Nigeria: Abu Musab al-Barnawi named as new leader." BBC News, August 3, 2016. http://www.bbc.com/news/world-africa-36963711

Ebiem, Osita. *Nigeria, Biafra and Boko Haram: Ending the Genocides Through Multistate Solution*. New York: Page Publishing, 2014.

Forest, James J. F. *Boko Haram in Nigeria Encyclopedia: Confronting Terrorism from the Islamic Sect, Threat to Homeland, Political History and Expansion, Attacks, President Goodluck Jonathan*. Smashwords Edition. Los Gatos, CA: Progressive Management, 2014. NOOK Book edition.

Joscelyn, Joseph. "A Well-Deserved Terrorist Designation." *The Weekly Standard*. November 13, 2013. http://www.weeklystandard.com/print/blogs/well-deserved-terrorist-designation_767037.html

Lee, Morgan. "Islamic Militants Hack to Death, Brutally Murder 106 Residents of Christian Farming Village in Nigeria." *The Christian Post*, February 18, 2014. http://m.christianpost.com/news/islamic-militants-hack-to-death-brutally-murder106-residents-of-christian-farming-village-in-nigeria-114692/

Martinez, Michael, Pierre Meilhan, and Faith Karimi. "'War on Boko Haram': African, Western nations unify in hunt for Nigerian girls." CNN, May 17, 2014. http://edition.cnn.com/2014/05/17/world/africa/nigeria-abducted-girls/

McCoy, Terrence. "The man behind the Nigerian girls' kidnappings and his death-defying mystique." *The Washington Post*, May 6, 2014. http://www.washingtonpost.com/news/morning-mix/wp/2014/05/06/the-man-behind-the-nigerian-girls-kidnappings-and-his-death-defying-mystique/?tid=hp_mm&hpid=z3

Moe, Alex. "Hillary Clinton: Kidnappings in Nigeria Are 'Abominable.'" NBC News, May 7, 2014. http://www.nbcnews.com/storyline/missing-nigeria-schoolgirls/hillary-clinton-kidnappings-nigeria-are-abominable-n99721

"Muslim group claims Nigeria blasts." *Aljazeera*, December 28, 2010. http://www.aljazeera.com/news/africa/2010/12/20101228123525363633.html

Naval Postgraduate School. *An Alliance Built Upon Necessity: Aqim, Boko Haram, and the African "Arch of Instability."* Charleston, SC: CreateSpace Publishing, 2014.

WORKS CONSULTED

Nossiter, Adam. "Tales of Escapees in Nigeria Add to Worries About Other Kidnapped Girls." *The New York Times*, May 14, 2014. http://www.nytimes.com/2014/05/15/world/africa/tales-of-escapees-in-nigeria-add-to-worries-about-other-kidnapped-girls.html?_r=0

Ogebe, Emmanuel. "More deadly than ISIS and al-Qaeda." World News Group, September 27, 2014. http://www.worldmag.com/2014/09/more_deadly_than_isis_and_al_qaeda/

Oteng, Mandy. "Buhari never said that war against Boko Haram is over—Adesina." Online Nigeria, December 27, 2016. http://news2.onlinenigeria.com/news/general/579587-buhari-never-said-that-war against-boko-haram-is-over-adesina.html

Perry, Alex. *The Hunt for Boko Haram: Investigating the terror tearing Nigeria apart.* London: Newsweek Insights, 2014. Kindle edition.

Simons, Richard. *Not with Our Daughters: Boko Haram & the Kidnapping of 300 Nigerian Schoolgirls: A New Pattern of Terror the World Must Unite and Stop.* Charleston, SC: CreateSpace Publishing, 2014.

Smith, David, and Harriet Sherwood. "Military operation launched to locate kidnapped Nigerian girls." *The Guardian*, May 14, 2014. http://www.theguardian.com/world/2014/may/14/nigeria-launches-military-operation-to-find-kidnapped-girls

Superville, Darlene. "Michelle Obama speaks out on kidnapped Nigerian schoolgirls." Associated Press, May 10, 2014. http://www.pbs.org/newshour/rundown/flotus-speaks-kidnapped-nigerian-girls/

U.S. Department of State, Bureau of Democracy, Human Rights and Labor. "Country Reports on Human Rights Practices for 2012: Nigeria." http://www.state.gov/j/drl/rls/hrrpt/humanrightsreport/index.htm?year=2012&dlid=204153

U.S. House of Representatives Committee on Foreign Affairs. *Boko Haram: The Growing Threat to Schoolgirls, Nigeria, and Beyond.* Washington, D.C.: U.S. Government Printing Office, 2014.

U.S. House of Representatives Committee on Homeland Security. *Boko Haram: The Growing Threat to U.S. Homeland.* Charleston, SC: CreateSpace Publishing, 2014.

Verini, James. "The War for Nigeria." *National Geographic*, November 2013. pp. 86–107.

Yan, Holly. "Nigeria abductions: 6 reasons why the world should demand action." CNN. May 6, 2014. http://www.cnn.com/2014/05/06/world/africa/nigeria-abductions-why-it-matters/

ON THE INTERNET

Salaam, Abeeb Olufemi. "The Psychological Make-up of Mohammed Yusuf." E-International Relations, November 4, 2013. http://www.e-ir.info/2013/11/04/the-psychological-make-up-of-mohammed-yusuf/

Terrorism Research & Analysis Consortium (TRAC). "Who is the real Abubakar Shekau (aka Abu Muhammad Bin Muhammad): Boko Haram's Renegade Warlord." http://www.trackingterrorism.org/article/who-real-abubakar-shekau-aka-abu-muhammad-abubakar-bin-muhammad-boko-harams-renegade-warlo-2

Zenn, Jacob, Atta Barkindo, and Nicholas A. Heras. "The Ideological Evolution of Boko Haram." *The RUSI Journal*, Volume 158, Issue 4, August 14, 2013. http://dx.doi.org/10.1080/03071847.2013.826506

INDEX

Abuja   14, 15, 24, 38
Adamawa   30
AK-47 (Kalashnikov)   7
Ansari, al-, Abu Usmatul   31
Ansaru   31, 33, 35, 37
Bama town   30
Bauchi   18, 26
Boko Haram   6, 7, 8, 9, 10, 11, 12, 13,
      15, 17, 18, 19, 21, 22, 23, 24, 25,
      26, 27, 28, 29, 30, 31, 32, 33, 34,
      35, 37, 38, 39
Borno   6, 12, 17, 18, 19, 27, 30
#BringBackOurGirls   12
Buni Yadi   34
Cameron, David   7, 13
Chibok   5, 6, 7, 8, 10, 11, 12, 13, 36,
      37, 38, 39
Clapper, James   35, 36
CNN   33
Christians   4, 7, 17, 18, 23, 31, 33
Clinton, Hillary   11
Doron Baga   32, 33
First and Second Deputy   21
Foreign Terror Organizations (FTOs)   33
Hausa   16, 17
Hollande, François   13
Igbo   16
improvised explosive devices (IEDs)   27
infidel(s)   22, 23, 25
Ishaku, Kuma   8
Islam   4, 17, 25, 28
Izghe   33
Jaji   29
jihad   17, 21, 22
Joint Task Force (JTF)   28
Jonathan, Goodluck   12, 24, 25, 27, 30,
      36, 37
Jonathan, Patience   36
Jos   23
Kaduna   28
Kano   18, 27, 30, 31
Lagos   5, 15
Local Cell Operational Commanders
      and Strategists   21
London   12, 13
Madalla   24
Maghreb   27, 28

Maiduguri   17, 19, 21, 22, 25, 28
Muslims   4, 5, 7, 17, 18, 23, 25, 31, 36
New York   4, 11, 12
Nigeria   5, 6, 7, 11, 12, 13, 14, 15, 16,
      17, 18, 19, 20, 22, 23, 24, 25, 26,
      27, 28, 29, 31, 32, 34, 35, 36, 37, 38
Nigerian Armed Forces   27
Nigerian Security Forces (NSF)   19, 35
Nur, Mamman   31
Obama, Barack   11, 13, 25
Obama, Michelle   11
Operational Cells   21
Paris   13
Plateau state   28
Potiskum   29
Qaeda, al-, Central (or Core al-Qaeda)
      22, 27, 28, 33
Qaeda, al-, in Iraq (AQI)   21
Qaeda, al-, in the Arabian Peninsula
      (AQAP)   28
Qaeda, al-, in the Islamic Maghreb
      (AQIM)   27, 28
Qaqa, Abu   28
RPG (rocket-propelled grenade)   7
Salafiyyah   17
Sambisa Forest   8, 9, 39
Shabaab, al-, in Somalia   28, 35
Sharia   18, 22
Shekau, Abubakar   6, 10, 12, 19, 21,
      22, 23, 25, 31, 39
Spiritual Leader   21
Shura Consultative Council   21
State Department   35, 37
State Operational Commanders and
      Strategists   21
State Security Service (SSS)   27
takfiri   22
Taliban   22, 33
United Nations   24
United Kingdom   15
United States   13, 35, 37
Wahhabites   17
West Africa   15
Yobe   18, 25, 27, 30
Yoruba   16
Yusuf, Mohammed   17, 19, 21, 22, 23,
      25, 31